COLOUR THEIR WORLD

Missing you

AUTHOR
ERICA LONDON

ILLUSTRATOR
MAYHARA FERRAZ

Dedication

*To my Dearest Uncle Paul, until we meet again.
My loving husband Mathew and our four beautiful
children. Remember, it's never too late to fulfill your
dreams.*

~Erica-Simone

*This book is for every little one who has a star shining
in the sky. Hope this brings warmth to your heart.*

~ Mayhara Ferraz

Where is my Uncle?
Where did he go?
Lord knows my heart
I miss him so

I checked the closet
Even knelt down to the ground
But you're nowhere to be found

Everyone is quiet with
nothing to say
Did you go on vacation
far far away?

Days have passed and
Saturday is here
Time to visit for our
family dinner
Is that crying I hear?

Mommy is crying and Auntie too
Uncle what have you done?
What's the matter with you?

They tell me you've gone
to a better place
No pain, no tears all
our fears erased

I hope it's true cause
I miss you so
No more hugs and kisses
No piggy backs in tow

The memories I will keep
for now and always
The jokes and selfies
Photographs for days
We say goodbye to a
man we all knew
Though you wouldn't be my
uncle if you didn't leave a clue

The whisper in the wind
The still gentle voice
You will never be far
I've given you no choice

For these games of hide and
seek we will always play
I'll be the winner when we
meet again someday.

Things to keep in mind...

- Tell your child the truth. No matter what age your child is, you should tell the truth about what has transpired right away. Not doing so, leaves room for speculation and doubts that may confuse your child even more.

- Deliver the news in doses. You know your child best. Share the news at a pace that gives them room to talk about and process what's happened. Some children may process the news right away, others take time. Some may express big emotions right away while some may react with no emotion at all. It's important to let your child know that the conversation doesn't end with one talk. Let them know that grief is a process and you are there to talk whenever they need to.

- Talk about feelings openly. Take time to explain and explore the different emotions involved in grief. Whether it's uncontrollable crying, overwhelming sadness or something more subtle, it's important for your child to understand that grief can come in a range of emotions. Encourage your child to process their feelings without embarrassment or fear of judgement.

- Make space for your child in the grieving process. Depending on how close they were to the deceased and their individual way of coping, being a part of the grieving process can actually help in your child's healing. Consider having your child choose clothing for the funeral, pick out a photo for a memorial or even choose a song that reminds them of their dearly departed loved one.

- Talk about the funeral.

- Funerals can be a confusing or sometimes scary experience for a child.

- Ask your child to describe what they saw to better understand how they viewed the experience and what stood out to them. Talk through their thoughts to help them process the experience in a positive way.

- Keep the conversation going about the deceased (as appropriate). If your child seems interested in doing so, talk about holidays or special moments that they shared with the deceased. This will jog their mind of special moments and may even initiate some humour in what could be a deeply emotional experience.

- Be open with your child on YOUR feelings. It's important for your child to see honesty in the way you process your grief. Show them it's normal and healthy to express their grief by expressing yourself in the way that best helps you. Cry out loud, scream out loud or even dance if it helps!

Conversation starters for you and your child

- How do you feel about_____ passing away?

- Where do you think they have gone?

- What are some things that you think you can do when you feel down?

- What are ways we can remember _____?

About the Author

After working in the medical field for over 20 years, juggling a fulfilling career all the while being a wife and mother of four, 2020 threw Erica for a loop as Covid caused this hard-working woman to have to choose between her career and her children.

Choosing her children, she put her teachers cap on grabbing any and everything, but a school bus.

Seeing how, writing has always been a passion of hers, all the scraps of pen to paper that was once thrown to the side have now become books of love.

About the Illustrator

Mayhara Ferraz is a Brazilian illustrator who currently lives in Portugal. She graduated with a degree in Visual Arts in Lisbon. This is where she rediscovered her passion for illustration and now shares her work with the world. However, being very specific as to the projects she takes on.

Giving colour to an author's story and bringing joy to little readers is what brings warmth to her heart. Besides illustrating Children's Books, she also spends her time creating characters, doodling, overthinking and doing personalized commissions with much love.

CPSIA information can be obtained
at www.ICGtesting.com
Printed in the USA
BVHW011232161121
621741BV00006B/78